D1231845

ST. MAARTEN/ ST. MARTIN

Photography by Hans and Pat Petruska

Introduction and copy editing by Stanley R. Larson

Pathans Publishing

Dedicated to Hans' Parents,
"OMA & APA" Johann and Magdalena Petruska

© 1991 by Pathans Publishing

To order additional copies, write the
publisher: Pathans Publishing,
9445 Olympia Dr. Eden Prairie,
Minnesota 55347 U.S.A.
612-942-5409   Fax: 612-942-0168

Acknowledgements:

To Mullet Bay Resort & Casino, Netherlands
Antilles, for permission to adapt some copy
from The Mullet Way, copyright 1988.

To Amy Kuphal for permission to use lines
from "Seaside Rendezvous," as captions for
plates 7 and 12, copyright 1991.

ISBN 0-936189-02-9

Printed in Hong Kong by Everbest Printing Co., Ltd.

To call Mullet Bay Resort & Casino from U.S.A.
DIAL 011-599-5-52801
P.O. BOX 309 MULLET BAY RESORT
ST. MAARTEN, NETHERLANDS ANTILLES

Introduction: the setting, the artists, the art

The Caribbean...

Mere mention of the phrase calls up images of sun and sea: sand beaches lapped by turquoise, white capped waves against the backdrop of volcanic and coral reef islands, lush and green and mountainous, under never-ending skies.

In fact, visitors often rightly describe the islands of the Caribbean as a 2000-mile-long string of jewels that curve from Florida to the northern coast of Venezuela, South America. Among these jewels emerging from the deep blue to emerald waters of the Caribbean is the island of St. Maarten/St. Martin.

Located at the northern end of the windward group of the Lesser Antilles, the hilly island gains the benefits of the prevailing gentle trade winds and warm seas that keep the average temperature around 80 degress. Here the Caribbean seems a tranquil sea, clearer, warmer, and less salty than the adjacent Atlantic. Its calm lagoons foster an atmosphere that draws people to enjoy the island's vibrant life.

Thirty-six beaches, all with public access, surround the island of St. Maarten/St. Martin, and each one displays such individuality that it seems as if it might have been created to satisfy a different desire.

Beautiful beaches draw sunseekers to long stretches of open space and powder-like sand. Sea grape trees give natural shade on some, while palm trees border others. Still other beaches, more secluded, seem protected by the rocky headland walls that frame a small cove offering quiet solitude. Dramatic limestone cliffs run the entire length of one narrow beach, while other shorelines lie within easy reach of hotels or resorts that offer every kind of watersport facility and equipment.

Always great for sun bathing and swimming, the clear radiant waters of St. Maarten also invite snorkelers and scuba divers to explore offshore coral reefs full of brightly colored fish and marine life. Divers and snorkelers can rent equipment at several places, including Mullet Bay Resort.

Adventurous islanders and visitors discover the delights of parasailing and gain an unparalleled view of the island from above. Experienced boardsurfers enjoy unlimited opportunities. First-time surfers may take advantage of lessons offered by watersports centers on the island. Those who have already acquired the skills and reflexes for jet skiing and water skiing enjoy both at Mullet Bay. Catamarans and trimarans provide afternoon sailing pleasure, or sunset and picnic sails, sport fishing, and intra-island excursions may also be arranged.

The best way to visit neighboring St. Barths or the Sandy Beach on Prickly Pear Island is to sail on the 53-foot Falcon or Bluebeard I & II. Inspiring visions of deserted coral isles unspoiled by time, Sandy Beach lies about four miles northwest of the British island of Anguilla.

A tiny sand bar island with a long beach, Prickly Pear is surrounded by a living coral reef, home of great varieties of tropical fish and other marine life in waist-deep to ten-foot-deep waters. Multiple hues of coral and shades of blue and aqua sea water and skies accent the dazzling white beach. And, as if not to be outdone by aquatic wonders, a rich intriguing mixture of tropical birds inhabit Prickly Pear Island.

But St. Maarten/St. Martin offers more than sunny beaches, recreation, and artistic inspiration.

The island covers about 37 square miles, and no barriers or border restrictions delay movement between the Dutch side and the French side, so sight-seers can travel the steep, winding roads of the entire island in half a day.

Shoppers find incredible offerings of quality and selection: clothing from the fashion capitals of the world; precision watches; gemstone jewelry; crystal; fabulous fragrances and cosmetics; Caribbean crafts and artwork; shoes, beachwear, and chic rare leathers; even video cameras and state-of-the-art electronics – all 100% duty free. The shopping plaza at Mullet Bay has several shops and boutiques, open until late hours every day. A shopper's delight.

Mullet Bay Resort, one of the Caribbeans most prestigious full service resorts, is located on the Dutch side, five minutes from Princess Juliana International Airport, accessed by major airlines.

Sun and surf make the perfect prelude to Mullet Bay's incomparable dining, and each tropic night brings an unmatched array of entertainment. Whether the vacationer wants a quiet, cozy hideaway or a lively party atmosphere, Mullet Bay has it all. The invitation is out for a spin of the roulette wheel or a deal of the cards at the Grand Casino, one of the island's largest.

Friends may decide to sip a cocktail in one of many lounges, party to the pulsating beat at Le Club, or take a romantic stroll under the stars.

Choosing the elegance of gourmet restaurants, diners savor the finest Chinese, French, Continental and Italian specialties. All cuisine, whether formal or casual, is expertly prepared.

Though a city all its own, 172-acre Mullet Bay Resort and Casino offers accommodations with a unique degree of privacy. Designed to suit the most discriminating traveler, the 600 luxurious rooms, one and two-bedroom suites and villas, offer the ultimate in comfort and convenience.

Mullet Bay's 18-hole championship golf course, designed by noted golf architect, Joseph Lee, is the only course on St. Maarten and one of the finest in the Caribbean. The course stands as a challenging masterpiece, a scenic wonder curving along the ocean, lagoon and hillsides.

Surfing or dining, relaxing on the beach or gaming at the Grand Casino, a Mullet Bay experience is one not easily forgotten!

Even history buffs will find fascination and interest in the story of St. Maarten/St. Martin. When Columbus "sailed the ocean blue," he may not have landed or even anchored here. But the great explorer paused long enough to name the island. He first sighted it on November 11, 1493, the feast day of St. Martin of Tours, a revered saint of Western Europe. So, for five centuries the island has been "on the map."

Arawak Indians originally populated the island, practiced agriculture and made pottery. Carib Indians from South America conquered the Arawaks shortly before the arrival of the Spaniards who occupied the island after Columbus.

The Spaniards used surviving Indians in forced labour until most of the Caribs perished in the mid-seventeenth century struggle between the French, English, Dutch, Danes and Spanish for control of the West Indies. For three centuries, pirates, privateers and smugglers plundered the islands and raided ships carrying cargoes of Mexican or Peruvian silver.

Between 1630 and 1648, the valuable trading and smuggling depots of Curacao, Saba, St. Eustatius and St. Maarten all came under Dutch control. On March 24, 1648, nine Dutch and French settlers negotiated an agreement for joint rule, and St. Maarten's territory was divided. The French gained about 21 square miles, and the Dutch kept sixteen. During various intervals from ten days to 180 years, the Netherlands, England, and France governed the island, and no government claimed the territory from 1690 to 1703. But the terms of the 1648 agreement included the principle that the people of St. Maarten/St. Martin will "live together in tranquility and help each other in time of need." The agreement has prevailed and survived.

Early settlers gave up their small tobacco farms and left the islands when labor proved too costly. Most island planters began growing sugar, importing West African slaves to work large acreages. Slaves soon outnumbered the European landowners. Growth in sugar, rum and slave trade and the high value of sugar duties drew the interest of European Colonial powers, so eighteenth century wars and treaties often involved transfers of West Indies Islands. Slavery was abolished by April 27, 1848. With cheap sugar available from other ports of the world, the economy on St. Maarten declined during the nineteenth century.

Now the richly diverse population totals about 25,000 on the Dutch side and 20,000 on the French side. Most islanders speak at least two languages. English is spoken nearly everywhere on the island. Visitors come from around the world, and St. Maarten/St. Martin, "the friendly island," welcomes them.

Here life flows at a slower pace. A favorite phrase heard
in this laid-back place is, "No problem!" People find
time to unwind. To sit back, reflect and gain a new
perspective on life.

No wonder award-winning photographic team Hans and Pat Petruska
return again and again to the tropical paradise of St. Maarten where they
find, during every season, another chance to create unique, exciting
photography.

For Hans and Pat, the mind and heart become the true lens of
the camera. Using combinations of light and composition, they have
come to know that a good photograph, like any other art form,
does not just happen. It is created. It is sought after. It
expresses their thoughts, their emotions, their sensitivities.

The pages of this book reflect the Petruskas' total commitment
to their art. Seeing photography as one of the most dynamic
forms of communication, they say that "unique photography
requires imagination, determination, and dedication . . .
The directions photography can take you are only limited by how
much you give of yourself and by the reach of your imagination."
The Petruskas' prove their theory in their work.

Roadmap St.Maarten

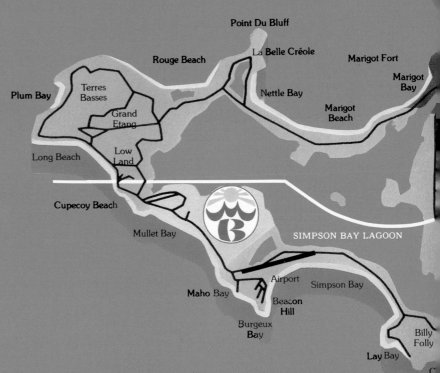

Fr

Potence Beach

Point Du Bluff

La Belle Créole

Marigot Fort

Rouge Beach

Marigot Bay

Terres Basses

Nettle Bay

Plum Bay

Marigot Beach

Grand Etang

Long Beach

Low Land

Cupecoy Beach

SIMPSON BAY LAGOON

Mullet Bay

Airport

Simpson Bay

Maho Bay

Beacon Hill

Billy Folly

Burgeux Bay

Lay Bay

C

CARIBBEAN SEA

North Point

Marcel Cove Beach

Bell Hill

French Cul De Sac

Grand Case

Grand Case Beach

Airport

Salines De
Grand Case

Orient Beach

Louis

Orleans

Rambaud

Etang Aux
Poissons

Paradise Peak

L'Embouchure Beach

FRENCH SIDE

Coconut Grove

Colombier

Maho
Well

French Quarter

ATLANTIC OCEAN

Marigot
Hill

Williams
Hill

St. Peter's

DUTCH SIDE

Dutch
Cul De Sac

Sentry
Hill

Prince's Quarter

Naked Boy
Hill

Cementary

Cole
Bay
Hill

Salt Pond

Guana Bay

Fort Hill

Fort
Williams

PHILIPSBURG

Cay
Bay
Hill

Pier

Bay

Little Bay

Great Bay

Fort Amsterdam

A.C. Wathey
Pier

Point Blanche Bay

Point Blanche

1 Juliana International Airport, situated
on the Dutch side, accommodates
many major airlines from the USA
and Europe.

2 (left) The 18-hole championship course at the 172-acre Mullet Bay Resort is the only golf course on the island. Eight of the holes border the resort's spectacular lagoon.

3 Sky and water seem determined to offer inspiration and beauty for islanders and visitors.

4 (left) Philipsburg, the capital of Dutch St. Maarten. In the foreground lies the great salt pond.

5 Cactus plants thrive in wild growth around the island.

6 What does an island boy dream as he ponders unlimited horizons on the magnificent Caribbean?

7 (right) Fun and sun at the deserted isla of Prickly Pear: "The whole world dances when the rocking waves roll in./The beach waits in a frenzy for the party to begin."

8 Little Italy restaurant at Mullet Bay, serves up tantalizing gourmet
   specialties.

9 The renown Building 90 suites overlooking the magnificent beach at Mullet Bay
   on the Dutch side of St. Maarten.

10 (left) Crystal clear, aqua blue waters lap the shores on the French side of St. Martin.

11 Cool tropical drinks please the eye and delight the taste buds.

12 Erich is having a ball in the water: "The wind pipes out delightful tunes, grabs a beach boy by the hand./A wink and they go waltzing, drop, bounce, skip across the sand./ Soon the surging sea spray woos him to forget the bounds of land."

13 (right) Vacationers go island hopping to neighboring St. Barths or head for Prickly Pear on one of the many catamarans available for island excursians.

14 The hillsides of St. Maarten blaze with color.

15 Hibiscus flowers grow in profusion all over the island.

16 (left) The Grand Casino at Mullet Bay, one of the largest casinos in the Caribbean, features both Atlantic City and Las Vegas style rules.

17 Every night in the Caribbean provides the ideal setting for romance.

18 Sun Worshipers at Prickly Pear Island.
19 (right) The Honeymooners walk at Mullet Bay starts at this
point, with the Caribbean waters running over the rocks.

20 Marigot offers a truly French experience of unique cafes, shops and market.

21 Cooling Caribbean rain drops refresh foliage.

22 A spectacular view from one
    of St. Maarten's beautiful
    private homes.

23 (right) Parasailers gain this
    perspective of St. Maarten's
    beaches caressed by Caribbean
    waters.

24 25 (overleaf)
    Oyster Pond enhances the
    beauty of a romantic evening,
    representing both the Dutch
    and French sides of the island.

26 (left) Elegant and tastefully decorated, the new state of the art 16,000 sq.ft. Conference Center at Mullet Bay is one of the finest in the Caribbean.

27 The Conference Center provides the ideal setting for both small and large groups.

28 Little Italy at Mullet Bay overlooks the fairways and lagoon.
29 (right) Nature and architecture join forces at Mullet Bay's magnificently appointed Building 90.

30 (left) The tennis village at Mullet Bay offers fourteen all-weather courts.

31 Wet bikes surrounded by magnificent landscaping in a natural inland lagoon.

32 St. Maarten is the habitat of dramatic flora and varieties of birds. Egrets may be seen all over the island.

33 The town of Orleans on the French side nestles into the hillside.

34 A beautiful villa with a magnificent view of St. Maarten from its mountain
vantage point.

35 St. Maarten never runs out of romantic settings.

36 37(overleaf) Mullet Bay's Championship Golf Course, designed by noted golf course architect Joseph Lee, offers a distinct challenge to the skilled professional and the best possible training ground for the novice.

38 39 Prepared with meticulous attention to detail, authentic Chinese delicacies are served and enjoyed in the unique ambience of the Bamboo Garden at Mullet Bay Resort.

40 Careful landscaping and stone
work surround some private
dwellings that dot the island.

41 (right) Shimmering effects
remain after a gentle-Caribbean
shower.

2 (left) No one ever tires of the surf and the sand, or the beautiful sandy beach at Prickly Pear Island.

3 ... who will walk this way with me, dreaming dreams of what might be ...

44 (left) Romance and the Caribbean are
synonymous.

45 The backdrop of the Caribbean combines
beauty and challenge for any golfer.

(left) A hazy day seems to whisper about peace and quiet on the tranquil island of St. Barths, a frequently chosen destination for excursions from Mullet Bay.

Every evening nature stages a repeat performance – always alike, always unique.

49 (overleaf) Aerial view of Mullet Bay Resort, combining the quiet moods of tropical paradise with the vibrancy of a country club.

50 (left) The Towers offers priviledged vacation ownership to those interested in investing in paradise.

51 Visitors and residents of the Towers enjoy unsurpassed views.

52 Watersports at Mullet Bay vary from deep sea fishing, to parasailing, sailboating, water skiing, jet skiing, scuba diving and snorkeling.

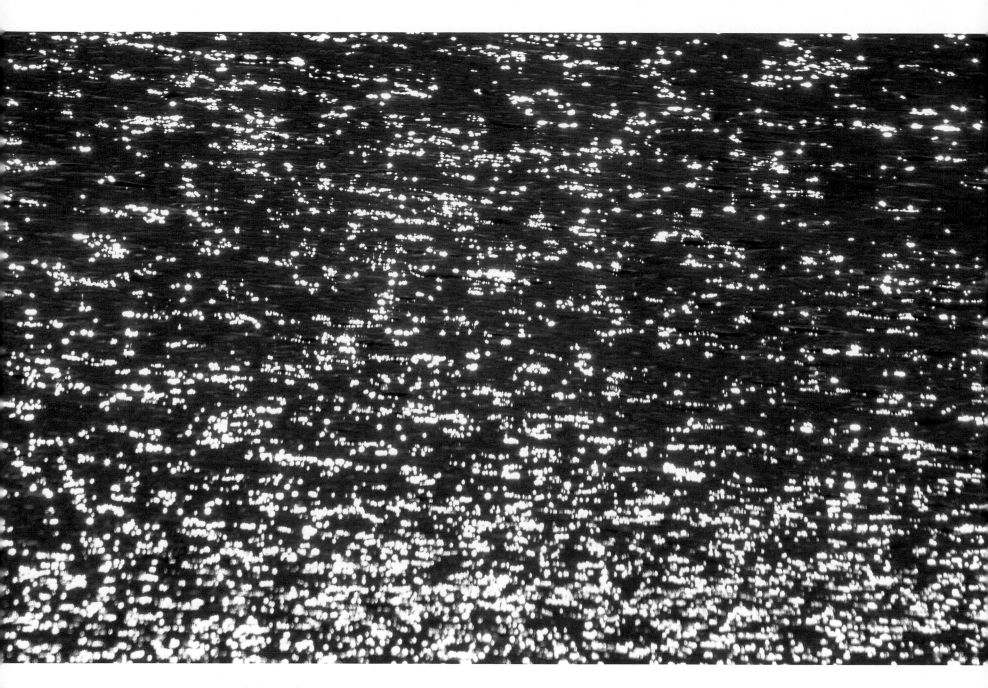

Textures of the Caribbean resonate with intensity.

54 A St. Maarten Islander.

55 Market in Marigot on Saturday
morning.

56 (left) The romantic oceanside pool at Mullet Bay Resort.

57 The exotic Bird of Paradise flourishes in it's natural environment.

58 The pier, where pirate vessels once moored offshore, now welcomes cruise ship passengers to shop on Front Street in Philipsburg and enjoy the friendly island of St. Maarten.

59 (right) Old boardwalk on golf course at Mullet Bay.

60 (overleaf) Another day on St. Maarten/St. Martin ends with the scintilating sweep of unforgettable hues in unmatched brilliancy.